I C

Embrace the

Wilderness

By Faith Phiri

Dedication

I would like to dedicate this book to **my parents**

Charles Phiri

Masiye Phiri

My young sister

Amina Phiri

and my fiancé

Greg Hunt

who have been there for me during my highest and lowest points in life. Who have supported me and encouraged me to continue to seek the favour of God. It is because of their encouragement and prayers that I am able to write this book.

Table of Contents

Introduction

Welcome. I am glad and delighted you have joined me to venture into hidden values of this book.

Have you ever had people tell you *"don't waste your wilderness experience"?* I have, I've heard sermons on it too, and for a while, it really encouraged me, but I want to be honest with you, it's hard sometimes. When you're in the wilderness, you feel so alone, you feel so helpless, you feel like you're going on an endless journey to nowhere, literally just wondering around in the wilderness with no destination. So, how can I embrace my wilderness experience?

How can I embrace my wilderness experience when it feels like it's sucking all the energy out of me, it's breaking my spirit, it's making me feel hopeless?

I've asked myself these questions many times, and today, I'm going to give you the answer the Lord told me. I am going to focus on the Israelite's journey to the Promised Land and their time in the physical wilderness.

How Can I Embrace the Wilderness?

When people would tell me to embrace my wilderness experience, I would often ask, *"Why should I? Is it really something I should be embracing? Don't you understand what I'm going through, why should I embrace this situation, for what"?*

I didn't understand why they said this, until now.

So, I'm here to tell you, **EMBRACE YOUR WILDERNESS EXPERIENCE.**

You're gonna ask me why aren't you? Hear me out!

Chapter 1: Check Your Foundation

Very often our life seems so amazing that we get wonderfully comfortable in the setting we are in, we get used to the routine and well, it seems great! But sometime God wants to shake things up a little bit, he wants us to move closer and closer to where he wants us to be and that means stirring things up a little, allowing life to happen, allowing storms to come our way.

Let me ask you something and be honest!

When life seems to be going amazingly well for you, how often do you seek God? How often do you just dwell in His presence?

I'll be honest, when I'm on cloud 9, I hardly spend time with God because all these good things are happening, instead of thanking God and giving Him the praise and worship he deserves, I tend to praise myself and my own efforts, forgetting that it was by God's power that all of this was possible!

I honestly feel like God wants to remind me that HE is in control and it is through HIM that all things are possible, it is not by my power but by HIS, it is not by my strength but by HIS strength. God wants to remind me where my help comes from and remind me to rely on Him and not on myself or the things of this world.

Now, from my experience, being in the wilderness normally comes when you least expect it, things look to be going great for you in life then something just hits you and everything is turned upside down, your husband/wife start acting strange, your job starts to stress you even more, your health suddenly starts to decline.... Things just don't go to plan anymore, and you wonder, WHY? Why is this happening to me? What have I done so wrong? Why does the enemy want to attack me? Why I'm I going through this? The **WHY** questions are always on our minds.

I had an experience like this, life just hit me, and I thought...why has this happened to me! My life was going so well! What sin have I committed that has caused me to hurt like this? What mean person has spoken evil against me and made me go through this! Why, Why, Why.

And instead of going to God, I decided to numb the experience, ignoring it until I found a solution! I watched Netflix and just kept myself busy so I wouldn't have to deal with the emotions.

Guys, have you ever been in situations where you are hurting so much but you have no one to reach out to? You can't speak to your friends, your family, your work colleagues, or church members? You feel so alone so you decide to numb the pain by supressing it or using other things to hide it, so you don't feel it like; Alcohol, sex, drugs, making yourself extra busy, even shopping. You want to escape the reality, so you try to temporarily delete it.

When I saw that things were just not going well for me, I started to get really angry at God! I would complain and complain until I got tired of hearing the same complaint coming out of my mouth. I never gave God the chance to respond, I wanted Him to do what I wanted.... but what I wanted wasn't what God wanted. What I thought I needed wasn't what I needed.

However, I didn't understand this because all I did was complain and cry. Many times, when situations happen, we spend a lot of time complaining to God, ranting, and shouting at Him. Asking Him why us, why do we have to go through this etc. We talk so much that we don't even give Him the chance to respond, we do our bit of talking then hang up the phone. We want God to intervene, but we don't give him the chance because we still want control and want things to go our way.

Is it that we are scared of the path God is going to take us on?

Guys, God is not trying to hurt you, quite the opposite actually. He wants to build your faith, help you become more mature, help you realise that you can't do anything except through Him.

Life will come at you and test your foundation! If your foundation is not secure, you will crash and fall, but if your life is built on a strong foundation, even when the wind blows, and waves crash on you, you will not fall.

Luke 6:46-48 says, *"Why do you call me, 'Lord, Lord,' and do not do what I say? As for everyone who comes to me and hears my words and puts them into practice, I will show you what they are like. They are like a man building a house, who dug down deep and laid the foundation on rock. When a flood came, the torrent struck that house but could not shake it, because it was well built".*

Storms reveal our foundation, you never know how well your house is built until it is tested. If your foundation is a little shaky, your faith will be shaken. When you feel overwhelmed, who will you cling to? The minute you wake up to the minute you go to sleep, you don't know what could happen. You're filled with doubt, fear, anger, frustration. So, in this time of fear, doubt, anger and frustration, who will you lay your foundation on?

God allows us to experience these wilderness moments to expose our foundations, to remind us that 'hey! Something ain't right here, you need to check your foundation'.

Verse 48 says the wise man laid his foundation on the rock. SO, who is your rock?

Isaiah 28:10 says *"Therefore, the Lord God said this, 'Look, I have laid a stone in Zion, a tested stone, a precious cornerstone. A sure foundation, the one who believes will be unshakeable".*

The torrent has come, it's shaking you, it's pressing you, it's trying to destroy you mentally, physically, emotionally, and spiritually. But who will you lay your foundation on?

We can be unshakeable if Jesus is our foundation

So, Build on Christ.

Jesus is your sure foundation in the storm, if you build your foundation on Christ, Hell can't come against you. If you put your faith in Him, he will never let you down.

Psalm 18:2 says, *"The lord is my rock, my fortress and my deliverer, my God is my rock, in whom I take refuge, my shield and the horn of my salvation, my strong hold".*

So, again, who will you lay your foundation on?

Matthew 7:25 says, *"The rain came down, the streams rose, and the winds blew and beat against that house; yet it did not fall, because it had its foundation on the rock"*

When life is going well and when life hits you like a wave, remember where your help comes from, remember who makes the impossible possible. *"With man, this is impossible, but with God, all things are possible"* - *Matthew 19:26.*

Life can get crazy but, we have peace. We can have peace in the midst of the storm. When our faith is built on the rock of Jesus Christ, we become unshakeable, there is no storm that can stop God from meeting your needs. Where there is shaking, an outpouring comes.

So, back to the question, 'Why should we embrace our wilderness experience?' Maybe God wants to expose your foundation, who are you clinging on when you feel overwhelmed? Where will you lay your foundation so that when the storm tries to break you, you will be unshakeable?

Chapter 2: Do You Believe?

Do you ever ask yourself how you ended up where you are? How have you ended up in this wilderness? Why you're here? I've asked myself those questions many times and sometimes it's hard to understand.

Often, situations hinder us from reaching out to the Father or when we do, we don't pray with faith and then the results are limited. Sarah Jakes Roberts put it perfectly when she said that we dilute our prayer requests with fear, anxiety, doubt, worry and insecurities. **Mark 11:24** says *"Therefore I say unto you, what things so ever ye desire, when ye pray, believe that ye receive them, and ye shall have them"*. We need to believe what we ask for from the Lord and believe that he is able.

Let's go to the New Testament quickly. Turn your Bibles to **Luke 4:49-56.** Remember Jairus's daughter, she was sick then, she died. **Verse 49** tells us that while he was speaking to Jesus, someone from the house came to Jairus and told him *"Thy daughter is dead, trouble not the Master"*. Brothers and sisters let me tell you something, there is going to be a voice that is going to try to convince you to give up your breakthrough, it'll try to convince you that it's too little too late, it'll try to convince you that this situation can't be brought back to life because it is dead! Jesus responded to Jairus because he knew he was about to be filled with thoughts of lies and in **verse 50 Jesus says,** *"Fear not: believe only, and she shall be made whole"*.

Isn't this amazing? Do you realise that belief can do wonders! Just because that situation seems dead to everybody else, that shouldn't change your prayer life! Pray and believe that God is able, pray and believe that God will come through, pray, and believe that you will see miracles happen, pray, and believe that breakthrough is coming!

Today is the day that you silence those voices of doubt, those voices of fear, and those voices of discouragement! They will tell you its dead, and how will you respond? My God has resurrecting power!

They will tell you its over, and how will you respond? My God will start a new thing!

They will tell you you're not good enough, you tell them, I am chosen by my Father in heaven, and he says I am worthy!

When they tell you to STOP bothering the teacher, START BOTHERING THE TEACHER! Because of that belief, child of God you will see miracles happen!

God is making a way for you; God is doing new things for you; you just need to believe it! Statistics may count you out, people may look down on you because of your age and people may look down on you because of the colour of your skin, your education or class. As a child of God, you serve a God who is a way maker, a miracle worker, a promise keeper, a light in your darkness! Get ready for overflow! He has done it before, and he will do it again. You must believe!

Mark 11:24 says "*Therefore I say unto you, what things so ever ye desire, when ye pray, believe that ye receive them, and ye shall have them*". Believe that you are so much more than you think you are, believe that your destiny is bigger than you know, believe that God has something supernatural and special waiting for you, and believe that God is taking you somewhere!

God has a call on your life brothers and sisters, and I know sometimes it may feel like you are just existing, trust me I feel that sometimes, but remember, God is changing you, he has bigger and better things installed for you. If you cooperate with God, even in your current circumstances, God will do something amazing in you! Read **Romans 8:18,** "*For I reckon that the suffering of this* *present time are not worthy to be compared with the glory which shall be revealed in us".* There's more for you child of God. Believe and receive it!

You are precious to your Heavenly Father, because of his love for you, you will **NEVER** be defeated!

Chapter 3: Pray Without Ceasing

How much do you pray when you're in the wilderness?

How much do you share your troubles with the Lord?

Do you tell him once and that's it?

If you do, why?

How do you expect God to bring breakthrough in your life if you're not going to him in prayer? You're forgetting that prayer is a powerful thing! Prayer isn't a minor thing that you just do in church or when you're about to eat. Prayer is a powerful thing! Prayer allows you to speak to your Father, to engage with your Father.

There are times that we pray and when we don't see results straight away, we give up! Guys! God's timing is the perfect timing, you must be patient, you must keep praying! Keep telling him what you need! He will answer in his timing! I read a powerful devotional on this on

YouVersion and they said, **"Bold prayers honour God and God honours bold prayers"**. Be persistent with your prayers. It doesn't matter if you don't see anything happen straight away, you keep praying, don't give up because God is going to come through!

You're in a wilderness right now correct? Why aren't you constantly praying!

You're in a storm right now correct? Why aren't you persistent in prayer!

You're in a desert right now correct? Why have you stopped praying!

Never Stop praying, never stop believing because our God is an awesome God who makes the impossible possible, he makes a way when there seems to be no way.

Exodus 14:13-14 reads, *"And Moses said unto the people, Fear ye not, stand still, and see the salvation of the Lord, which he will shew to you today: for the Egyptians*

whom ye have seen today, ye shall see them again no more forever. The Lord shall fight for you, and ye shall hold your peace". Moses reminded the Israelites that they should put their hope in God, they should pray continually because God was about to give them the breakthrough they so desperately prayed for. God had heard and answered them!

Do you believe he can answer you as well?

When we continue to look to God, our perspective on things start to change, we start to see things through God's eyes and not our human eyes. The thing that we thought was impossible is now possible because of the hope we have, because of the faith we have in our Father.

I know we can all become self-reliant and want to take matters into our own hands but let me ask you something, don't you feel hope when you look at an impossible situation and remember that you have a saviour who can make the impossible possible? I sure do, when I face impossible situations, I just speak to those situations and tell them, *"God will deal with you!"*. No matter how scary the situation is, the Holy Spirit always reminds me that my God is able!

Can I get an Amen please!

No matter how fearful I am, the Holy Spirit reminds me that my God is with me, he will never leave me nor forsake me! I speak the words of **Psalm 23.**

Today, I want you to read those words and really believe them because the Lord is your shepherd.

"The Lord is my shepherd; I shall not want. He maketh me to lie down in green pastures: he leadeth me beside the still waters. He restoreth my soul: he leadeth me in the paths of righteousness for his name's sake. Ye, though I walk through the valley of the shadow of death, I will fear no evil: for thou art with me; thy rod and thy staff they comfort me. Thou preparest a table before me in the

presence of mine enemies: thou anointest my head with oil; my cup runneth over. Surely goodness and mercy will follow me all the days of my life: and I will dwell in the house of the Lord for ever".

I believe those words with my whole heart. I honestly believe the Lord is my shepherd because of everything he has done for me in my life. Even when I feel the urge to gravitate towards my own understanding, I remember those words of **Proverbs 3:5-9** *"Trust in the Lord with all thine heart; and lean not unto thine own understanding. In all thy ways acknowledge him, and he shall direct thy paths. Be not wise in thine own eyes: fear the Lord and depart from evil. It shall be health to thy navel, and marrow to thy bones. Honour the Lord with thy substance, and with the first fruit of all thine increase: So, shall thy barns be filled with plenty, and thy presses shall burst out with new wine. My son despise not the chastening of the Lord, neither be weary of his correction.*

For whom the Lord loveth he correcteth: even as a father the son in whom he delighteth".

No matter how many times I try, life always reminds me that I can't control anything. God is in control. That's why he asks us to go to him with our requests, to seek him, to knock on his door and just say *"God I can't do this alone, I need you!"*. I assure you brothers and sisters, your Father in heaven will come through for you, coming through in ways you wouldn't imagine!

Rejoice always, pray without ceasing, and give thanks to God in every circumstance. **2 Corinthians 12:9** *"And he said unto me, my grace is sufficient for thee: for my strength is made perfect in weakness. Most gladly therefore will I rath glory in my infirmities, that the power of Christ may rest upon me"*. Let go and let God, then you will see his power made perfect in your weakness.

Pray with boldness, when you're faced with trouble, pray with boldness. Those who pray for boldness acknowledge that they are in the midst of a challenge, they are vulnerable so they know they need protection, they need a place where they can find refuge. *"Taste and see that the Lord is good, blessed is the one who takes refuge in him," Psalm 34:8 NIV.* Pray that fear will not overcome you, pray for boldness, troubles will come, but, you can take refuge in God.

Chapter 4: Long or Short Route?

If you're anything like me, you probably hate being in the wilderness, you probably hate going through struggles because you feel so helpless, you feel alone, you feel worthless. You would rather be in a position of comfort than in the midst of a storm, right?

Think back at the Israelites when they were brought into the wilderness after God freed them from the hands of the Egyptians. They probably felt the same way. Suddenly, they're in this wilderness, not enough food, or water and are expected to just survive. The scriptures tell us that they wished they were back in Egypt. **Exodus 16:3** *And the children of Israel said unto them, Would to God we had died by the hand of the LORD in the land of Egypt, when we sat by the flesh pots, ana when we did eat bread to the full; for ye have brought us forth into this wilderness, to kill this whole assembly with hunger".* They wished they had died by God's hands in Egypt where they had a comfortable life even though they were not free.

Don't we ever feel like this? God instructs us where to go and when we feel we won't be able to survive, we decide it is better to stay in that comfortable place of suffering?

But isn't being in the wilderness beneficial for our spiritual growth? It is in the wilderness that we really seek God, it is in the wilderness that we are brought to our knees. The wilderness experience humbles us. Go to the book of **Deuteronomy 8: 2-3** *"And thou shalt remember all the way which the Lord thy God led thee these forty years in the wilderness, to humble thee, and to prove thee, to know what was in thine heart, whether though wouldest keep his commandments, or no. And he humbled thee, and suffered thee to hunger, and fed thee with manna, which thou knewest not, neither did thy fathers know; that he might make thee know that man doth not live by bread only, but by every word that*

proceedeth out of the mouth of the Lord doth man live".
When we go through the wilderness, God humbles us and by this, I mean, we realise we don't have the capabilities to handle this by ourselves, we realise it is by the power of God that we are saved, only God himself can save us and thus becoming dependant on Him.

Very often we feel so overwhelmed by our circumstances that we forget this, and so did the Israelites sometimes. Can we really get out of this? We are in the middle of nowhere, can God really handle this? Why is God taking us this way? A lot of these questions were probably running through their minds and honestly, the same questions run through my mind when I'm in the wilderness experience. There have been times in my life where I have questioned God, I doubt if He can get me out of this wilderness because in my eyes, it doesn't look possible, the fight is too big that my human eyes make me feel like this issue is too big for God to handle. I'm sure if

I were in the wilderness with the Israelites, I would struggle to grasp what was going on as well, why go the long way when we can go the short way? Why go through the desert where there is no provision for food and water when we can go the short way and have access to all of this in a shorter amount of time? Why does God want us to go through the struggles of the long road when we can have the comfort of the short road?

Brothers and sisters, while we're in the wilderness, God may take us out using the long route because the short route is full of dangers. **Exodus 13: 17-18** *"And it came to pass, when Pharaoh had let the people go, that God led them not through the way of the land of the Philistines, although that was near; for God said, Lest peradventure the people repent when they see war, they return to Egypt"*. I know this verse is a little difficult to understand so let me explain. God took the Israelites the long way despite the other way being shorter because of the dangers that they would face. If the people were to face war, they would have changed their minds and returned to Egypt, not fully trusting in the Saviour who took them out of Egypt. At the first sight of war, they would be running back to their oppressors and not the Lord. So instead, God took them the long way so He could ready them for battle and what a battle they did fight! So, as Rabbi Kirt Schneider says *"Don't waste your wilderness. What you receive in your wilderness is going to bless you for the rest of your life".*

The Israelites wondered in the wilderness for 40 years, 40 YEARS! That was a long time, but God was working in them. He was preparing them to enter the Promised Land as in their current state, they wouldn't be able to manage in the land of Canaan. In our current state, we wouldn't be able to manage or cope in the place God wants us to be in. So, God needs to work in us, He needs to do some serious heart surgery, some character development, work on our trust issues, work on our commitment issues. God needs to work on a lot of things in us.

Now guys, this process is painful! God will make you confront yourself; he will make you confront your emotions; he will make you confront your sins. He will make you confront the hurt and it is so painful.... These are the times I cry myself to sleep. It has taken a long time for me to be where I am today. I couldn't have started writing books like this if God hadn't taken me through periods of being in the wilderness. If you have read Upfront Faith, you have seen how much of a wreck I was growing up, God took me by the hand and told me we were going on a retreat and it would be painful. Change requires stripping away the old self and putting on the new self, it requires putting to death your fleshly desires and seeking first the kingdom of God. Guys do you know how hard that was for me? Giving up the pleasures of the world? It was hard. There were times I would rebel and go my own way and I would enjoy myself immensely, I would have the time of my life, but God would always be knocking on the door of my heart.

I remember when life hit me the hardest and I was in this wilderness experience that felt like it would never end. God would always tell me that before he could bring me to the fullness of my inheritance, he first had to humble me. He first had to make me realise that I needed to depend on him. But obviously I was going through such a hard time so I would ignore God and just cry out *"Lord, Lord! Why Am I here? Why Am I going through this? How will I get through this? Why me? What should I do Lord?"*. And he would always respond with the same answer, to humble me and be dependent on him.

For God to bring me out of this wilderness, he had to strip me bare and make me reliant on him and him alone, in the current state I was in, I wasn't able to do that. When trouble came, I would have doubted him and continued my complaining. But, let me tell you something amazing! It'll bring joy to your heart I promise. It's in the wilderness that we often experience the supernatural provision of God!

Go with me to **Exodus 16:2-4.** *Verse 2-3 "And the whole congregation of the children of Israel murmured against Moses and Aaron in the Wilderness. And the children of Israel said unto them, Would to God we had died by the hand of the Lord in the land of Egypt, when we sat by the flesh pots, and when we did eat bread to the full; for ye have brought us forth into this wilderness, to kill this whole assembly with hunger".* Even though God was with them, they still complained and didn't trust him enough to provide for them. Then God did something incredible! Read **verse 4,** *"Then said the Lord unto Moses, Behold, I will rain bread from heaven for you; and the people shall go out and gather a certain rate every day, that I may prove them; whether they will walk in my law, or no".*

While the children of Israel were complaining, brothers and sisters, God already had a plan to satisfy their hunger! He was bringing food from heaven!

Brothers and sisters, when we are busy complaining about how tough the wilderness experience is and planning on ways, WE can get out of it and how WE can provide for our needs, God already has it covered. He has already gone before you and provided for you before you have even asked Him. We are so busy complaining and worrying instead of looking up to heaven. God does amazing things for us while we are in the wilderness, things that we thought were impossible, He makes possible, when we think there is no way, God makes a way. God brought bread from heaven, **BREAD FROM HEAVEN!** Can you make bread from heaven? No! Only God!

God has done supernatural things for me in my life. Here are a few stories:

When I was younger, God spoke to me one night, I had a dream and I heard, clear as day, the name Emmanuel and what does Emmanuel mean? God with us! I woke up, brushed it off and went on about my day. The next night, I heard the name Samuel which means God has heard or Name of God. Samuel was also the prophet that anointed King Saul and King David if you remember, this is especially important in the story. So, again I brushed it off. Then suddenly, a wilderness came my way! I didn't know how to get out of it. I was only in college at the time. Then I remembered the dream I had. Emmanuel, God with us. I smiled so much because I knew that God was telling me prior that he was with me no matter the season. Then Samuel, God heard my prayer and then what happened next! Your girl was anointed!

I will forever remember this moment because that day, I heard the voice of God loud and clear right before the wilderness.

The next story was when I was living in Wolverhampton. My whole time in Wolverhampton was a time when I was in the wilderness. No matter how much I tried, I just couldn't escape the wilderness. My parents tried so hard to get me home but, I would always refuse even though I knew Wolverhampton was not the place for me. Again, if you have read Upfront Faith, you will know the types of shenanigans I got up to. Of course, my parents didn't know what I was up to but like Job, they were praying for me just in case I had sinned. **Job 1:5** "*And it was so, when the days of their feasting were gone about, that job sent and sanctified them, and rose up early in the morning, and offered burnt offerings according to the number of them: for Job said, It may be that my sons have sinned, and cursed God in their hearts. Thus, did Job continually*".

Brothers and sisters, my parents prayed just in case prayers for me and their prayers followed me to

Wolverhampton. I may not have been praying for myself, but they were praying for God's protection over my life. Now, this one night, I knew that God had heard their prayers. I was asleep one night and I had the most terrifying dream. In the dream I saw a demonic figure disguise itself as one of my loved ones. It made me feel comfortable with it being around because I thought it was one of my family members. Suddenly, it sat on my bed, got a light, and started shining it in on my face but I never saw its face. Then it lowered itself toward my ear and whispered, *"Your soul would have died if I tried to get in"*. Immediately, I had sleep paralysis and I felt this thing on me. I cried out to God in fear and I woke up straight away. I was so terrified that I started to pray and pray and after that encounter, I started to pray every night before going to bed for God to protect my sleep.

Now, the thing I want to emphasise is that this demonic force said *"your soul <u>would</u> have died"* meaning, God's hand of protection was already upon me and my parents. God was already protecting me from the powers of darkness. He provided protection before this demonic force tried to attack me. And my parents trusted God fully that he would protect me.

Brothers and sisters, if only we could trust in God a little more and know His character, we wouldn't approach our wilderness experiences with so much negativity. Instead, we would learn to embrace them and understand that there is a purpose for the wilderness. God wants you to learn something from this experience. If He can bring manna from heaven for the Israelites, he can bring manna from heaven for you. Don't underestimate the power of God.

Chapter 5: God will Provide

Many times, in the Bible, we see how God provides for his people not only for food, but with victory over tough situations. Gideon was able to defeat the enemy with only 300 men in **Judges 7.** Even though he was afraid, God came through for him, God had already given them victory over the enemy. Go to **Judges 7:13-15** *"And when Gideon was come, behold, there was a man that told a dream unto his fellow, and said, Behold, I dreamed a dream, and, lo, a cake of barley bread tumbled into the host of Midian, and came unto a tent, and smote it that it* *fell, and overturned it, that the tent lay along. And his fellow answered and said, this is nothing else save the sword of Gideon the son of Joash, a man of Israel: for into his hand hath God delivered Midian, and all the host. And it was so, when Gideon heard the telling of the dream, and the interpretation thereof, that he worshipped, and returned into the host of Israel, and said, Arise; for the LORD hath delivered into your hand the host of Midian.*

God came through for his children. Again, in **Deuteronomy 20:1-4** *"When thou goest out to battle against thine enemies, and seest horses, and chariots, and a people more than thou, be not afraid of them: for the LORD thy God is with thee, which brought thee up out of the land of Egypt. And it shall be, when ye are come nigh unto the battle, that the priest shall approach and speak unto the people, And shall say unto them, Hear, O Israel, ye approach this day unto battle against your*

enemies: let not your hearts faint, fear not, and do not tremble, neither be ye terrified because of them; For the LORD your God is he that goeth with you, to fight for you against your enemies, to save you.

The Lord always provides a way for us, no matter how impossible it may seem, the Lord will make a way. There are times we see our situations as beyond repair, or we are in situations that are so overwhelming and you feel like the Israelites in Deuteronomy, you see your enemies and they are larger that you could ever imagine, they are ready for battle, they are ready to hit you with all they have, and they know they will win because there is one of you and many of them. At this point, you feel helpless, you don't have the resources, you don't have the time, you don't have the skills, everything you wanted is not happening and you cry out to God asking for him to intervene because the enemy is ready to destroy you.

But child of God, as the Lord said to the Israelites, today you will go into battle with your enemies, with your fears, with your anxieties, with your insecurities, with your circumstances! Today, you will go to war! But do not be afraid, do not be faint-hearted; do not panic or be terrified by them why? *For the LORD, your God is he that goeth with you, to fight for you against your enemies, to save you.* The Lord will provide victory for you, he is Yahweh Yireh, the Lord who provides, Yahweh Nissi, The Lord our banner. Child of God there is a banner of victory over your head. Moses says in **Exodus 17:15-16 NIV** *"The Lord is my Banner"* and in the KJV *"And Moses built an altar, and called the name of it Jehovahnissi"*

Brothers and sisters, I want to give you some words from God that will remind you that he is The Lord who provides:

1. Philippians 4:19 *But my God shall supply all your need according to his riches in glory by Christ Jesus.*

2. Psalm 81:10 *I am the L<small>ORD</small> thy God, which brought thee out of the land of Egypt: open thy mouth wide, and I will fill it.*

3. Psalm 84:11 *For the L<small>ORD</small> God is a sun and shield: the L<small>ORD</small> will give grace and glory: no good thing will he withhold from them that walk uprightly.*

4. Psalm 18:1-2 *I will love thee, O L<small>ORD</small>, my strength. The L<small>ORD</small> is my rock, and my fortress, and my deliverer; my God, my strength, in whom I will trust; my buckler, and the horn of my salvation, and my high tower.*

5. Jeremiah 29: 11 *For I know the thoughts that I think toward you, saith the LORD, thoughts of peace, and not of evil, to give you an expected end.*

6. Matthew 7:7-8 *Ask, and it shall be given you; seek, and ye shall find; knock, and it shall be opened unto you: For everyone that asketh receiveth; and he that seeketh findeth; and to him that knocketh it shall be opened.*

7. John 15: 7 *If ye abide in me, and my words abide in you, ye shall ask what ye will, and it shall be done unto you.*

8. 2 Corinthians 9: 8 *And God is able to make all grace abound toward you; that ye, always having all sufficiency in all things, may abound to every good work:*

No matter what the wilderness is throwing at you, remember the one thing that always rings true, God is going to provide for you and make a way for you. Even if the circumstance is shouting GIVE UP, IT'S OVER!

Don't stop fighting.

Believe.

Chapter 6: We Find Our Purpose in the Wilderness

So, we find purpose in the wilderness huh?

Do you believe that?

If you don't, why don't you?

If you do, why do you?

I'm asking because I'm curious, maybe one day, if God wills it, we can all meet up and have this discussion.

Let me tell you what I think. I 100% believe we can find purpose in our wilderness experiences and here's why. My wilderness experience made me who I am today. I **was** once a wild child with "don't care" attitude and God really humbled me. Now, when I say humbled, I mean humbled!! I used to be a selfish individual and God put me in my place. I was reading the book of **Hosea 12:8-9 NIV** *"Ephraim boasts, I am very rich; I have come wealthy. With all my wealth they will not find in me any iniquity or sin".* Then the Lord responds with the most amazing statement in verse 9 *"I have been the Lord your God, ever since you came out of Egypt; I will make you live in tents again, as in the days of your appointed festivals".* Guys when I read that, I remembered myself and I felt those words! ***"I will make you live in tents again".***

He showed me the reality of life, he showed me how my actions affect others, he showed me how my attitude and actions affect my parents, my sister, my family. My wilderness experience helped me with my character, it helped me confront a lot of bad habits and behaviours I had. If it weren't for those wilderness experiences, I wouldn't be writing this book right now. I don't even want to think about where I'd be.

But it's because of the things that God taught me and showed me in the wilderness that made me the person I am. I saw God's power, I heard him speak. He showed me where I'd be if I didn't change. I couldn't go backwards now, I had to keep going forward and I decided, I had to keep going with God. Start with God, continue with God and finish with God. I wasn't going to give up, I would keep going, and obeying God's every command. When I kept my eyes fixed on God, I tell you what, I started to understand my purpose in life because

God was revealing it to me. I wasn't put on this earth just for just, I was put on this earth for a greater purpose! And so are you!

The wilderness experience will expose a lot of things! God will show you wonders! It is in the wilderness that I remembered that I wanted to work with the youth, to be an influencer, to be an ambassador for Christ. Then God started to put opportunities on my lap. University, placement, preaching opportunities, masters, ambassador for a youth organisation, writing a book, getting involved in evangelism on social media! There was a purpose for my wilderness experience...and I see it now. Keep your eyes fixed on Jesus and you will see great things.

God used the wilderness experience to forge my identity just like he did for the Israelites. They went through hardships and God made them go through this to prepare them for the Promised Land. **Deuteronomy 8:2-3** *"And thou shalt remember all the way which the Lord thy God*

led thee these forty years in the wilderness, to humble thee, and to prove thee, to know what is thine heart, whether though wouldest keep his commandments, or no. And he humbled thee, and suffered thee to hunger, and fed thee with manna, which though knewest not, neither did thy fathers know; that he might make thee know that man both not live by bread only, but by every word that proceedth out of the mouth of the Lord doth man live".

Does that make any sense? The Israelites needed to be able to check their own hearts and fully be in partnership with God, depending on him. God made them go through all of that hardship to build them up, so they could realise that it was not by their own power that they left Egypt, survived in the wilderness 40 years, and entered the Promised Land. No, it was by the power of God that all this was possible, it is because they trusted that he would lead them. When we read more, we see that other started to find out about what God had been doing for his people, the wondrous things he did for them! Go to the book of **Joshua 2:9-10** "*And she (Rahab) said unto the men, I know that the Lord hath given you the land, and that your terror is fallen upon us, and that all the inhabitants of the land faint because of you. For we have heard how the Lord dried up the water of the Red sea for you, when ye came out of Egypt; and what ye did unto the two kings of the Amorites, that were on the other side of the Jordan, Sihon and Og, whom ye utterly destroyed".* The Israelites had a testimony to testify! They started to fulfil God's purpose in their lives.

Your wilderness experience may not be pleasant; however, God has not forgotten you, he is preparing you, building you, healing you, sanctifying you. God is working in your life brothers and sisters. Whatever experience you are going through right now, God is using that to work out his purpose in you. There is a purpose for your wilderness experience.

Brothers and sisters, I know it's hard but let me tell you something I heard by **Bianca Olthoff,** our purpose will come out of the pressing moments in life. It is our struggles of life that produce the greatest harvest, the fruit that will last. Look at the Lord Jesus Christ when he was in the garden of Gethsemane. Go with me to **Mark 14:33-36,** *"And he taketh with him Peter and James and John, and began to be sore amazed, and to be very heavy; And saith unto them, My soul is exceeding sorrowful unto death: tarry ye here, and watch. And he went forward a little, and fell on the ground, and prayed that, if it were possible, the hour might pass from him. And he said, Abba, Father, all things are possible unto thee; take away this cup from me: nevertheless, not what I will, but what thou wilt".*

Brothers and sisters, we serve a God who knows our every fear, anxiety and worry because he felt it. He prayed to the Father saying Father, take this cup from me. Jesus was going through something here, he was scared, he was troubled, he felt sorrow, he felt what you feel right now but! He knew that this pressure would not crush him, so he stayed under that pressure because a miracle was going to happen.

You may feel like you are being hit on every side, you're being crushed, beaten, battered and sometimes you feel like no one understands but remember, Jesus understands because he felt it! He knows what you are going through, the fear, anxiety, and worry. He knows the feeling, but you need to do as Christ did and that is, *"Not what I will, but what thou wilt",* let God move the way he will move, you have to let God press you to bless you. This wilderness experience will not break you; it will make you. You need to follow Christ to where he is calling you even if that means walking into the wilderness, but if you keep your eyes on Christ, you will see your purpose come out. It is God's will, not our own.

You want your anointing, but you don't want to pay the price for it, if you can't handle the pressing, you can't handle the anointing. God will make a way in the wilderness; you will see streams come through where you thought was a dry waste land. Your wilderness experience is going to transform you.

Chapter 7: Stop Grumbling

Do you all remember when the Israelites were about to go into the Promised Land? Moses sent some people to explore the land and see if the people who lived there were strong or weak, this is when we come to the feedback in **Numbers 13:26 onwards.**

"And they went and came to Moses, and to Aaron, and to all the congregation of the children of Israel, unto the wilderness of Paran, to Kadesh; and brought back word unto them, and unto all the congregation, and shewed them the fruit of the land. And they told him, and said, we came unto the land whither thou sentest us, and surely it floweth with milk and honey; and this is the fruit of it.

Nevertheless, the people be strong that dwell in the land, and the cities are walled, and very great: and moreover, we saw the children of Anak there. The Amalekites dwell in the land of the south: and the Hittites, and the Jebusites, and the Amorites, dwell in the mountains: and the Canaanites dwell by the sea, and by the coast of Jordan. And Caleb stilled the people before Moses, and said, let us go up at once, and possess it; for we are well able to overcome it. But the men that went up with him

said, we be not able to go up against the people; for they are stronger than we. And they brought up an evil report of the land which they had searched unto the children of Israel, saying, the land, through which we have gone to search it, is a land that eateth up the inhabitants thereof; and all the people that we saw in it are men of a great stature.

And there we saw the giants, the sons of Anak, which come of the giants: and we were in our own sight as grasshoppers, and so we were in their sight".

They saw danger and were ready to give up because it was impossible! I mean, they had every right to feel that way, if we saw the dangers that lay ahead, I would probably feel the same way. BUT they forgot something important! Wasn't it God that parted the red sea for them? THE RED SEA! Wasn't it he who sent manna from heaven, meat from heaven? Wasn't it God who brought you out of your previous circumstances? Wasn't it God who saved you from that situation that could have taken your life? Wasn't it God that gave you that job that you thought was impossible to get? Wasn't it God who brought finances when things just seemed impossible?

Like the Israelites, we often forget the miracles that God did for us, the showers of blessings that he pours on us. Instead, we sit there grumbling and complaining and often say things that we don't mean. The Israelites did the same thing, they grumbled and complained. **Numbers chapter 14:1-4 reads:**

"And all the congregation lifted up their voice and cried; and the people wept that night. And all the children of Israel murmured against Moses and against Aaron: and the whole congregation said unto them, Would God that we had died in the land of Egypt! or would God we had died in this wilderness! And wherefore hath the LORD brought us unto this land, to fall by the sword, that our wives and our children should be a prey? Were it

not better for us to return into Egypt? And they said one to another, let us make a captain, and let us return into Egypt".

They were ready to give up, they completely disregarded everything God had done for them and as soon as they sensed danger or saw danger, they started to treat God like he was worthless or beneath consideration. They questioned him, doubted him. They had no faith. They wanted to go back to Egypt where they would be slaves or possibly killed, just so they could have that "comfortable" life. Are there times when you feel like that? You're in this wilderness experience and God shows you the path to take and it seems so impossible and dangerous, so you decide to take the easy road? Well, this is what the Israelites wanted. Let's continue, **verse 5-10 reads:**

Then Moses and Aaron fell on their faces before all the assembly of the congregation of the children of Israel. And Joshua the son of Nun, and Caleb the son of

Jephunneh, which were of them that searched the land, rent their clothes: And they spake unto all the company of the children of Israel, saying, The land, which we passed through to search it, is an exceeding good land. If the LORD delight in us, then he will bring us into this land, and give it us; a land which floweth with milk and honey. Only rebel not ye against the LORD, neither fear ye the people of the land; for they are bread for us: their defence is departed from them, and the LORD is with us: fear them not. But all the congregation bade stone them with stones. And the glory of the LORD appeared in the tabernacle of the congregation before all the children of Israel.

These men had faith in God, they had seen how God had protected them and provided them all this time and they knew he would continue to do so. Our God is a God who keeps his promises. The Lord told his people that he would deliver them from the Egyptians, and he did, but many people failed to see this. Even when Joshua and Caleb tried to encourage them, the people had already made up their mind and didn't want to hear anything they had to say, in fact, they wanted to stone them. So, God confronted them.

Verse 11-19 *"And the LORD said unto Moses, how long will this people provoke me? And how long will it be ere they believe me, for all the signs which I have shewed among them? I will smite them with the pestilence, and disinherit them, and will make of thee a greater nation and mightier than they. And Moses said unto the LORD, Then the Egyptians shall hear it, (for thou broughtest up this people in thy might from among them;) And they will tell it to the inhabitants of this land: for they have heard that thou LORD art among this people, that thou LORD art seen face to face, and that thy cloud standeth over them, and that thou goest before them, by daytime in a pillar of a cloud, and in a pillar of fire by night. Now if thou shalt kill all this people as one man, then the nations which have heard the fame of thee will speak, saying, Because the LORD was not able to bring this people into the land which he sware unto them, therefore he hath slain them in the wilderness. And now, I beseech thee, let the power of my lord be great, according as thou hast spoken, saying, The LORD is longsuffering, and of great mercy, forgiving iniquity and transgression, and by no means clearing the guilty, visiting the iniquity of the fathers upon the children unto the third and fourth generation. Pardon, I beseech thee, the iniquity of this people according unto the greatness of thy mercy, and as thou hast forgiven this people, from Egypt even until now.*

Moses had to speak on behalf of the Israelites because God had had enough! He did all these signs and wonders for them and still they wouldn't believe in him. They see danger and instead of turning to God, they turn away and try to take matters into their own hands (trying to get back to Egypt), or they just complain and grumble. Let's carry on because it gets better.

Verse 20 – 27 *"And the LORD said, I have pardoned according to thy word: But as truly as I live, all the earth shall be filled with the glory of the LORD. Because all those men which have seen my glory, and my miracles, which I did in Egypt and in the wilderness, and have tempted me now these ten times, and have not hearkened to my voice; Surely they shall not see the land which I sware unto their fathers, neither shall any of them that provoked me see it: But my servant Caleb, because he had another spirit with him, and hath followed me fully, him will I bring into the land whereinto he went;* **and his** *seed shall possess it. (Now the Amalekites and the Canaanites dwelt in the valley.) Tomorrow turn you and get you into the wilderness by the way of the Red sea. And the LORD spake unto Moses and unto Aaron, saying, how long shall I bear with this evil congregation,* *which murmur against me? I have heard the murmurings of the children of Israel, which they murmur against me.*

Guys do you see how our disbelief and distrust hurts God? God will do so much for us, clear a path for us, the promise land is right in sight, the miracle is there, ready for us to grab but as soon as we sense danger we want to run. We ask God why he is doing this, why is he taking us this way, why this why that. We complain instead of positioning ourselves to receive the blessings God has for us. You want to know something heart breaking? As I was reading **verse 24,** I nearly cried, the NIV version says this, *"no one who has treated me with contempt will see it".* That verse hit me hard! I had to sit back and really take in what I was reading. I searched the word *"contempt"* to find its meaning, and this is what it means, *"the feeling that a person or a thing is worthless or beneath consideration".* Brothers and sisters, do you ever consider that God can truly get you out of the wilderness?

Do you ever consider that he is able? Or do you feel it is worthless calling out to him because the situation is too much, or you complain to him for getting you to that place? When we grumble and complain like that, have you ever considered how your heavenly Father feels?

Now, I want to remind you of something, remember when the Israelites started talking about going back to Egypt and saying if only, they had died in Egypt, they said they God was going to cause them to die etc. Well, God heard their cries and complaints. **Verse 28-38** *"Say unto them, as truly as I live, saith the LORD, as ye have spoken in mine ears, so will I do to you: Your carcases shall fall in this wilderness; and all that were numbered of you, according to your whole number, from twenty years old and upward which have murmured against me. Doubtless ye shall not come into the land, concerning which I sware to make you dwell therein, save Caleb the son of Jephunneh, and Joshua the son of Nun. But your little* *ones, which ye said should be a prey, them will I bring in, and they shall know the land which ye have despised. But as for you, your carcases, they shall fall in this wilderness. And your children shall wander in the wilderness forty years, and bear your whoredoms, until your carcases be wasted in the wilderness.*

After the number of the days in which ye searched the land, even forty days, each day for a year, shall ye bear your iniquities, even forty years, and ye shall know my breach of promise. I the LORD have said, I will surely do it unto all this evil congregation, that are gathered together against me: in this wilderness they shall be consumed, and there they shall die. And the men, which Moses sent to search the land, who returned, and made all the congregation to murmur against him, by bringing up a slander upon the land, Even those men that did bring up the evil report upon the land, died by the plague before the LORD. But Joshua the son of Nun, and Caleb the son of Jephunneh, which were of the men that went to search the land, lived still.

Because of their disobedience, doubt and distrust in the Lord, God told them, they would not reach the Promised Land instead, they would wonder in the wilderness for 40 years until those 20 years and over died. Because of their disbelief, they ended up causing themselves to wonder the wilderness longer! Careful what you say guys, the tongue holds the power of life and death! The Israelites sealed their own fate, their doubt blocked their blessings.

Do we often block our own blessings? Do we sabotage our own miracles? I want you to think about this carefully brothers and sisters because this will determine whether you receive your breakthrough or not. Don't underestimate God.

Brothers and sisters, even when things don't look possible, trust in God! Even when things don't look doable, trust in God, even when you feel there is no way, trust in God because God can do miracles! If he can raise the dead, part the sea, give sight to the blind, make the lame walk, heal the sick, remove demons, turn water to wine, feed the thousands not once but TWICE! HE CAN MOVE IN YOUR SITUATION! It may take time but, God's timing is the perfect timing! Don't be disheartened! Our God is able.

Finally, **verse 39- 45 reads** *"And Moses told these sayings unto all the children of Israel: and the people mourned greatly. And they rose up early in the morning, and gat them up into the top of the mountain, saying, Lo, we be here, and will go up unto the place which the LORD hath promised: for we have sinned. And Moses said, wherefore now do ye transgress the commandment of the LORD? but it shall not prosper. Go not up, for the LORD is not among you; that ye be not smitten before your enemies. For the Amalekites and the Canaanites are*

there before you, and ye shall fall by the sword: because ye are turned away from the LORD, therefore the LORD will not be with you. But they presumed to go up unto the hilltop: nevertheless, the ark of the covenant of the LORD, and Moses, departed not out of the camp. Then the Amalekites came down, and the Canaanites which dwelt in that hill, and smote them, and discomfited them, even unto Hormah.

The Israelites realised what they had done, and they mourned, instead of going to God, they decided to get up in the morning saying, 'yeah now we are ready to enter the Promised Land, we have recognised that we have sinned", this was after God had told them they would not enter the Promised Land! Because of the consequence of their actions and words, they thought if they changed their mind-set, God would still allow them to go into the Promised Land but no, did they go to God with true repentance or false repentance? Did they just recognise their sins after God told them he wouldn't let them set foot into the Promised Land? If you don't know the difference between true repentance and false repentance, be sure to check out my book Upfront Faith to find out more.

When we continue to read on, we see that Moses tells the Israelites that it's a little too late now, they are again disobeying God's commandments by going up to the mountain, to do what? What exactly do they possibly think will happen once they get there? God's hand is not upon them, they have turned from him. But they didn't want to listen now did they? So, they went up and what happened, in their presumption, they went up that hill country, I'm sure they were walking with such confidence, but neither Moses nor the ark of The Lord's covenant moved from where they were. They went by themselves. God said no and they said go. Then the enemy who lived on that hill country came down and basically attacked them and killed them. Because of their disobedience, doubt, grumbling, disbelief, their turning away from God. God was not with them and they fell by the sword.

Has this ever happened to you? God says one thing and you do another, do you ever prevail? There have been times when I have tried to do things even though God said no and it has failed, so now, I make sure I listen and obey every word that the Lord says! And how do I know that it is God, well because I recognise his voice the way you would recognise your mum, dad, or sibling's voice when they called you, because you have a close relationship. I know his character; I have a close relationship with him, so I recognise him when he calls. I urge you to do the same.

Let me ask you something, do you like being patient? I need to ask because I'm the most impatient person, I want things to happen now, I struggle when it comes to being patient and very often in my suffering, I'm sure God gets tired of me always nudging him asking **"are we there yet, how long left, is the blessing coming today, when is it coming"**? He has had to sit me down and have a serious talk with me. This was like a Father Daughter talk. He has been teaching me that I need to be patient in my suffering, to get over what I am under, I need to be patient. But not only this, he has been telling me to rejoice in my suffering. Now, when I think of that I'm like, **"you said what now?"** How can I rejoice in my suffering, why should I rejoice?

Go to **James 1:2-8**, "*My brethren, count it all joy when ye fall into divers' temptations; Knowing this, that the trying of your faith worketh patience. But let patience have her perfect work, that ye may be perfect and entire, wanting nothing. If any of you lack wisdom, let him ask of God, that giveth to all men liberally, and upbraideth not; and it shall be given him. But let him ask in faith, nothing wavering. For he, that wavereth is like a wave of the sea*

driven with the wind and tossed. For let not that man think that he shall receive any thing of the Lord. A double minded man is unstable in all his ways".

I won't lie, I didn't understand what any of this meant so I asked God and he told me. I was watching a sermon by **Bianca Olthoff** and this is what she said. The Israelites said, **"Lord we don't want to be slaves anymore we want to be free",** God gave them their freedom and when they couldn't handle the wilderness and all its lows, they said they wanted to go back to Egypt because they faced hardships. Then they complained that they wanted food and God gave them food, but they got tired of it, they just complained but here, **James 1:2** is telling us to count it all joy.

Sometimes our wilderness experiences make no sense, things just don't add up and we start asking a lot of WHY questions, but **James** tells us to evaluate our struggles from the standpoint of joy, we don't understand what God is

72

doing but we need to choose to believe that what he is doing is for my good and for his glory. **Romans 8:28** *"And we know that all things work together for good to them that love God, to them who are the called according to his purpose"*. God makes all things work together for my good.

Hebrews 12:2 says, *"Looking unto Jesus the author and finisher of our faith; who for the joy that was set before him endured the cross, despising the shame, and is set down at the right hand of the throne of God"*. He didn't have joy for the crucifixion, he had joy for the resurrection. Our outlook will determine the outcome of the situation, our attitude will determine how we approach something and how we will accomplish it. It's not about our feelings because our feelings will come and go, it's all about the decision we are going to make, the will to believe and trust that God is in control.

Brothers and sisters, perseverance while in the wilderness means never giving up! If we continue to read on in **James 1**, we see in **verse 5** that **James** says we need to ask God for wisdom and then in **verse 6**, "*But let him ask in faith, nothing wavering. For he, that wavereth is like a wave of the sea driven with the wind and tossed*". Then **verse 8** "*A double minded man is unstable in all his ways*". What exactly does this mean, this type of person is a split personality Christian as **Bianca Olthoff said**, they are the ones that say I believe in God's will and his plan for my life but then they also say, I don't know if God speaks. They want to have it their way and God's way, but they can't. They want God to move but they still want control of their lives. How can God move when you are holding on to things in your life? How can God move in your life if you won't let him be in the driver's seat? How can God move in your life if you think your way is better than God's way? You can't have half commitment and expect a full blessing. God's in control. Not my will, but your will Lord. Let me leave you with the words from **verse 12:**

"Blessed is the man that endureth temptation: for when he is tried, he shall receive the crown of life, which the Lord hath promised to them that love him"

Chapter 8: Position Yourself to Receive the Miracle

One of my favourite worship songs is Miracles by Jesus Culture. The lyrics are so accurate and remind me of the nature of God. Whenever I hear that song and I'm faced with hardship, I listen to the words and I speak into that situation to remind it of the God I serve!

Brothers and sisters, miracles still happen, God still does miracles. You must believe. No matter how impossible, God will make it possible. No matter how dead it is, God will bring it to life. Look at the book of **Ezekiel** and the story of the dry bones in **chapter 37.** God is able.

I want to take you to the book of Joshua, right before they entered the Promised Land. But before that, just a little back story, so in **chapter 2,** here we see Joshua has sent spies to have a look around the place and they meet

Rahab, we've already read this previously. Now, she had told them that their enemy is filled with fear because they know of what God has done for them and they have basically already taken the city! So, the Israelites now know that the Lord is surely with them and they prepared themselves to receive the promise!

Now we go to **Chapter 3 and verse 5** *"And Joshua said unto the people, sanctify yourselves: for tomorrow the LORD will do wonders among you"*. The Israelites were preparing themselves; they were purifying themselves. They were getting ready to leave behind all their sin and baggage in the wilderness so that once they crossed over to the promised land, none of their past would go with them. Look at the word sanctify, what does it mean? Well, it means holiness, and therefore, to be sanctified means to be made holy, clothing yourselves with God's nature and by doing that, you understand his character, you trust and obey him in every season because you know his character, you are in relationship with him. To be sanctified is to be made into the nature of God and this is why God told them to sanctify themselves, they had to leave their sinful nature behind, they could not step into the promised land until they purified themselves because they were about to start a new life, their old baggage could not enter the promised land with them.

Moving on to **verse 6 – 17** *"And Joshua spake unto the priests, saying, take up the Ark of the Covenant, and pass over before the people. And they took up the Ark of the Covenant and went before the people. And the LORD said unto Joshua, This day will I begin to magnify thee in the sight of all Israel, that they may know that, as I was with Moses, so I will be with thee. And thou shalt command the priests that bear the Ark of the Covenant, saying, when ye are come to the brink of the water of Jordan, ye shall stand still in Jordan.*

And Joshua said unto the children of Israel, come hither, and hear the words of the LORD your God. And Joshua said, Hereby ye shall know that the living God is among you, and that he will without fail drive out from before you the Canaanites, and the Hittites, and the Hivites, and the Perizzites, and the Girgashites, and the Amorites, and the Jebusites. Behold, the ark of the covenant of the LORD of all the earth passeth over before you into Jordan. Now therefore take you twelve men out of the tribes of Israel, out of every tribe a man. And it shall come to pass, as soon as the soles of the feet of the priests that bear the ark of the LORD, the LORD of all the earth, shall rest in the waters of Jordan, that the waters of Jordan shall be cut off from the waters that come down from above; and they shall stand upon a heap.

And it came to pass, when the people removed from their tents, to pass over Jordan, and the priests bearing the ark of the covenant before the people; And as they that bare *the ark were come unto Jordan, and the feet of the priests that bare the ark were dipped in the brim of the water, (for Jordan overfloweth all his banks all the time of harvest,) That the waters which came down from above stood and rose up upon an heap very far from the city Adam, that is beside Zaretan: and those that came down toward the sea of the plain, even the salt sea, failed, and were cut off: and the people passed over right against Jericho. And the priests that bare the ark of the covenant of the LORD stood firm on dry ground in the midst of Jordan, and all the Israelites passed over on dry ground, until all the people were passed clean over Jordan.*

It was time for the Israelites to enter the Promised Land! They had sanctified themselves and they were in the position to receive the Promised Land. The people put all their trust in God. They knew they would be able to cross over the Jordan river and they took a leap of faith! The priests took a step into the river and a miracle happened!

The water from upstream stopped flowing, it piled up in a heap a distance away and I'm sure many people saw it! People saw the Lord come through for his children! They saw the power of the Lord Almighty.

If only the generation before had the same faith, they would have been able to witness this wonderful moment again! And when I say again, I mean the same miracle (Red Sea) different generation. No matter what, the children of Israel trusted God, they kept their faith. God always keeps his promises even if they take longer to come about, but he keeps his promises. He had fulfilled the promise he made to Abraham.

Do you believe God can still do a miracle in your life?

Are you willing to leave behind the past and your sins and trust God fully?

Are you ready to take a leap of faith and step into the Jordan river?

Have you positioned yourself to receive that breakthrough?

Chapter 9: Can I Make It?

- Do you think you will make it through whatever situation you are in?
- Do you think you can make it to the end?
- Can you start with God, continue with God and finish with God?
- After reading everything we have discussed, do you believe that you can make it through this situation?

If you said yes to those questions, good! Because the answer should be yes!

I want to take you to the book of **1 Samuel 17,** David defeating Goliath. People really questioned if David could defeat Goliath because of his size, age, and because he was not a soldier. Even before that, the Israelites were afraid and possibly even questioned if they would make it, **verse 11 says** *"When Saul and all Israel heard those words* of the Philistine, they were dismayed, and greatly afraid". They were afraid, if we read the description of Goliath, he sounds like a very scary individual, how could they face him? They would be defeated straight away! Then David came along and what did he do, he told them they could make it, they would defeat the Philistines because God was with them. Look at **verse 37**, "*David said moreover, The LORD that delivered me out of the paw of the lion, and out of the paw of the bear, he will deliver me out of the hand of this Philistine. And Saul said unto David, Go, and the LORD be with thee*". David knew God's character, God had delivered him from the paw of the lion and the bear, so he knew he would deliver him from the Philistines. He had faith; he knew he could make it!

There are times people will doubt you or when you try to face your circumstances, they mock you just as Goliath mocked David in **verse 43-44.** They try to make you feel inferior, they try to make you feel worthless, useless, and powerless. *"And the Philistine said unto David, Am I a dog, that thou comest to me with staves? And the Philistine cursed David by his gods. And the Philistine said to David, come to me, and I will give thy flesh unto the fowls of the air, and to the beasts of the field"*. Let me ask you something, how do you think David and the Israelites felt when Goliath cursed at them, cursed at God?

Go to **Proverbs 18: 21** *"Death and life are in the power of the tongue: and they that love it shall eat the fruit thereof"*. I don't even want to imagine what Goliath was saying to the people, but I can imagine it wasn't nice, he was definitely not blessing them or giving them words of encouragement, no, quite the contrary. Now I want to ask you something, when someone is going through a tough time, what words do you use on them? Words of encouragement or discouragement? Words of compassion or hate? Or what words are used on you and how do they affect you?

The words that come out of our mouths or the words that we hear coming out of other people's mouths about ourselves create a reality that we inhabit either for the better or the worst, they shape our lives and our experiences. Our words can either bring life or damage a person. Saul and his army probably let Goliath's words get to them and they probably felt extremely discouraged and maybe Goliath thought he would achieve the same thing with David. Can you imagine what would have happened if Goliath's words got to David, can you imagine if he just gave up, what kind of future would the Israelites have faced?

There is power in the words we speak, and it has the power to change the direction of our lives, so, who is directing the direction of your life, God, or man? God or your struggles?

God was directing the direction of David's life and God was continuously encouraging him, reassuring him, strengthening him and because of this, David didn't let the words of Goliath affect him, he was not disheartened, instead, he faced the situation head on. David faced Goliath even though he was insulting him and cursing at him. He faced Goliath knowing that God was with him and knowing that God would deliver the Philistines into his hands.

Verse 45-51 *"Then said David to the Philistine, Thou comest to me with a sword, and with a spear, and with a shield: but I come to thee in the name of the LORD of hosts, the God of the armies of Israel, whom thou hast defied. This day will the LORD deliver thee into mine hand; and I will smite thee, and take thine head from thee; and I will give the carcases of the host of the Philistines this day unto the fowls of the air, and to the wild beasts of the earth; that all the earth may know that* there is a God in Israel. And all this assembly shall know that the LORD saveth not with sword and spear: for the battle is the LORD's, and he will give you into our hands. And it came to pass, when the Philistine arose, and came, and drew nigh to meet David, that David hastened, and ran toward the army to meet the Philistine. And David put his hand in his bag, and took thence a stone, and slang it, and smote the Philistine in his forehead, that the stone sunk into his forehead; and he fell upon his face to the earth. So, David prevailed over the Philistine with a sling and with a stone, and smote the Philistine, and slew him; but there was no sword in the hand of David. Therefore, David ran, and stood upon the Philistine, and took his sword, and drew it out of the sheath thereof, and slew him, and cut off his head therewith. And when the Philistines saw their champion was dead, they fled".

Isn't this amazing! The faith David had in God, knowing he could do it no matter what? Knowing God would come through, knowing he could make it!

This is the same attitude we need to have, never allowing people to discourage us, never letting our circumstances intimidate us. We need to face those situations with faith knowing God will come through for us. It's not the size of the weapon that matters brothers and sisters, it's the size of faith in God that matters because God is bigger than all our problems, he is bigger than any storm that comes our way, he is bigger than any Goliath that comes our way and he will deliver us!

It's ok not to be ok, life can become bitter, it's hard, we were not promised an easy road, struggles will come, we will go through trying moments, but the decisions we make today will determine our tomorrow. If we read the book of **Ruth,** Ruth and Naomi didn't know that God was going to move the way he moved in their lives, he did the impossible, Ruth married Boaz and then she got pregnant! She was infertile but God performed a miracle and she conceived. God did what others said was impossible! When life sucks brothers and sisters, don't give up, GET UP! Things will happen that you might say are a coincidence, but they are all in God's plan, just look to him. Your end might just be your beginning.

Chapter 10: Where Do You Find Your Peace?

This section is going to be short but, I want to get straight to the point! I had a problem of going to other sources to get peace. When I was filled with so much sorrow and worry, my go to was often watching Korean Dramas which I absolutely love! But I found that every time I felt anxious, I found peace in that. However, it wasn't giving me peace, it was just my way of numbing my pain and forgetting about it for a while. Once the show ended, those anxious thoughts would come back and then I'd watch another show. I would spend the whole day watching them.

Now, I'm not saying watching Korean Dramas is bad, it's about balance, but for me personally, after reflecting on myself more, I found that I couldn't hide from my problems, I couldn't numb them because they would always be there. However, I could give them to God and ask him to give me peace.

I was reading the book of Jeremiah 17:5 and it reads *"Thus saith the LORD; Cursed be the man that trusteth in man, and maketh flesh his arm, and whose heart departeth from the LORD".* I started to wonder, did I put my trust in man? Did I draw strength from mere flesh? Now, I am not cursed as in the cursed that we think of today, that is not what Jeremiah is saying here. Here is what it means in biblical terms. I love watching Transformation Church and I remember hearing one of the pastors explain what this idea of "cursed" means. He said cursed just means you are left to your own devices, you're in the state you were in when you were born, you're in the natural pain that you experience on this earth. You have no hope for the future. You have decided that this fallen world can give you the "peace" that you so badly desire but because it is a fallen world, you will probably endure more pain. I did. The pain never went away, the hurt never went away, in fact, it became worse! Nothing in this world can give you the peace that the Lord gives. **Verse 7 of Jeremiah 17 says** *"Blessed is the man that trusteth in the LORD, and whose hope the LORD is".* No matter what happens in life, you have decided that you will make the Lord your hope and your confidence.

Now, I'm going to get real with you guys! How many times have you said, "Lord I trust you" and then tried to take control of the situation or you've turned from God's ways? If you say you haven't done that then I know you are lying because we all do! I've done it many times and it is only now that I am learning that peace doesn't mean taking control, when I say "Lord I trust you" it doesn't mean I take control. It's an act of surrender. Surrendering all to God and saying to him, "Lord have your way! Not my will but your will be done". Brothers and sisters let me tell you something, you can tell God all day long that you trust him but, we see the fruit! God will say to us, "I hear you, but I also see what you are doing", (I got that from a sermon from Transformation Church) but, what he said is accurate! Our actions don't match what we are saying to God and this is a problem. God wants to give us a peace that surpasses all understanding and we're like "Yes, yes we receive it Lord" but then, our actions start to tell a different story.

We need to stop telling God one thing and then we start doing another. There is a real disconnect between what we want God to do in our lives and what it will take for that to come to pass. We tell God we want to be stronger but we don't want to go through the struggle, we want to go deeper in our relationship with God but we don't want him to disrupt our schedule. Make it make sense.

Chapter 11: Remember the Faithfulness of God

Mark 8:19-20

"When I brake the five loaves among five thousand, how many baskets full of fragments took ye up? They say unto him, Twelve.

And when the seven among four thousand, how many baskets full of fragments took ye up? And they said, Seven".

If God did something amazing once in your life, he could do it again! He parted the red sea and then the Jordan river. If he did it once, he can do it again. Don't let the difficulty of the wilderness experience make you doubt the faithfulness of God. You know the history you have with God, he has come through for you before, so why doubt him?

Remember the faithfulness of God. We look at how big the problem is and end up asking the wrong questions.

We get worried and anxious why? Again, because we are asking God the wrong questions. Look at **Matthew 6:31-33** *"Therefore take no thought, saying, what shall we eat? or, what shall we drink? or, Wherewithal shall we be clothed? (For after all these things do the Gentiles seek:) for your heavenly Father knoweth that ye have need of all these things. But seek ye first the kingdom of God, and his righteousness; and all these things shall be added unto you".* Worry is connected to asking the wrong questions, all those **"What if"** questions. You need to ask the right questions. Remember when Jesus fed the 5000 in **Mark 6:38,** what did he ask? ***He saith unto them, how many***

loaves have ye? This question doesn't lead to worry, it leads you to start looking. It's not about what you lost, it's about what God has given you and what you still have left.

Sometimes it's so much easier to complain about what you don't have instead of what God has given us already.

I want to remind you of another important thing brothers and sisters. If you want to see miracles happen in your life, you need to start getting compassionate! Why? Because compassion activates the miraculous as **Pastor Robert Madu** said. Sometimes we pray for miracles that only benefit us but, **Pastor Robert Madu says, "You're called to problems because you're called to people. Compassion is when care and action collide"**. We need to care about others beside ourselves.

Some of you are in this wilderness season and you feel like you are being broken but do you know why God is breaking you, because he is about to use you like you have never been used before. He is about to do wonders for you, your life is about to change, you're going to reach people, people will be saved because of you. That's why you can't quit brothers and sisters, don't quit, keep going, remember the faithfulness of God, he's done it before he can do it again. It's hard I know, I'm going through it myself but, trust in God.

So, how are you going to respond to God today? Because remember, a response can push you towards your destiny. I'm not talking about how you are going to react, no, I'm talking about how you are going to respond, there's a big difference. Your reaction involves your emotions, are your emotions, always right? Have you ever reacted to someone and thought "my goodness I wish I never said that"? I have many, many times and it's because I reacted with my emotions. I didn't respond, I reacted! So, again, how will you respond to God today?

How will you respond to your wilderness experience?

Psalms 46

God *is* our refuge and strength, a very present help in
trouble.
Therefore we will not fear, even though the earth be
removed,
And though the mountains be carried into the midst of
the sea; *though* its waters roar *and* be troubled, *though* the
mountains shake with its swelling. *Selah*

There is a river whose streams shall make glad the city of
God, The holy *place* of the tabernacle of the Most High.
God *is* in the midst of her, she shall not be moved; God
shall help her, just at the break of dawn. The nations
raged, the kingdoms were moved; He uttered His voice,

the earth melted. The LORD of hosts *is* with us; The God of Jacob *is* our refuge. *Selah*

Come, behold the works of the LORD, who has made desolations in the earth. He makes wars cease to the end of the earth; He breaks the bow and cuts the spear in two; He burns the chariot in the fire. Be still and know that I *am* God; I will be exalted among the nations, I will be exalted in the earth! The LORD of hosts *is* with us; The God of Jacob *is* our refuge. *Selah*

Printed in Great Britain
by Amazon

58967877R00059